GNAWED BONES

Peggy Shumaker

Gnawed Bones

POEMS

 RED HEN PRESS | Los Angeles, California

Book design by Wanda Chin.
Cover image © Barry McWayne.
Author photo by Barry McWayne.

Library of Congress Catalog in Publication data:

Shumaker, Peggy
Gnawed bones
ISBN: 978-1-59709-156-5 (paperback)
1. Poetry—mortality 2. Family 3. Title
2009930459

The Annenberg Foundation, the California Council on the Arts, the James
Irvine Foundation, the Department of Cultural Affairs / City of Los Angeles,
the National Endowment for the Arts, and many individual donors generously
support Red Hen Press.

Published by Red Hen Press
www.redhen.org

First Edition

for Joe

TABLE OF CONTENTS

I I . *MYSTERY AISLE*

III. *OUR MOTHER OF SORROWS*

GNAWED BONES

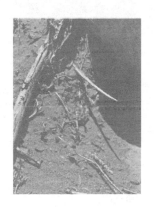

I. JULY TWILIGHT ON THE CHENA

JULY TWILIGHT ON THE CHENA

Red fox on the riverbank
leaps downed birch—
two, three—
what he's after
scrambling, invisible
from our riverboat.

Red fox, skinny
shins flailing,
dives out of sight. Moist
dirt shelters him,
absorbs the inked tip
of his lavish tail.

His secrets are his. Bright
salmon—breaching!—keep
secrets too. Beavers chew
vein-rich silver alder,
every mouthful a word,
a world untold.

WHAT WE GET USED TO

Bent forelegs first young
four-point buck settles

belly first on blades
sun-warmed, gone to seed.

One striped ear bends,
swivels toward laughter.

Back hoof split stretches over
tawny shoulder to scratch

inside his ear's
wide plush tunnel—

he's unafraid
of poetry, unafraid of this

itch we can't reach, itch
we can't stop.

Sounds inside a shaking head
head shaking hard to rout

that buzz, that torment,
winged voices taking off.

ORCAS ISLAND

SEA CHANGE

Solar wind takes two days
    to reach us,
oval aurora throbbing, sun
    more agitated
this year than last.

Ice walkers see
through the thinning pack
    seal shadows gliding.
Daggers of oil slip
    between our ribs.

We have some serious
vanishing to do.

AFTER DA-KA-XEEN MEHNER'S SCULPTURE
WEAPON OF OIL

SNAPSHOT

Feral pigs hook tusks, uproot
ti leaves, leave unbound
to earth a shock of red ginger.

Mongoose nip
windfall papaya, rip
stems of staghorn fern.

Flightless birds
have no chance
to walk away.

Giant ferns unfurl,
open hairy
fiddleheads to wind-

born o'hia.
Invaders always take
more.

Under jagged
rivers of lava,
new earth builds,

vents, runs fire makai,
spumes acid
and steam

poisonous, full
of promise—harsh
as any beginning.

POLISHED TABLE

When this koa tree stood,
honeycreepers nested among its burls,
hopped and waddled where they wanted
to go, tightroped along roots
stretched over forest floor.

When this koa tree fell,
mongoose darted nest to nest.
At twilight, stowaway rats
nosed windfall guava,
papaya, passionfruit.

Feral pigs yanked out
tender fiddleheads, new shoots
of ti, o'hia, maile.
When this koa was milled,
the honeycreeper's song

echoed—laughter of cousins
splashing barefoot in ocean,
children long gone, dressed
in the long sleeves of their lives,
their eyes now and then closing

to let in the song
of winged ones
unnested, gone.

DELIVERANCE

after Chagall

What kind of Moses
would arrive in the form
of a rooster tall enough

to brush his comb
along the doorjamb,
his arched back

a feathered saddle
iridescent?
One roll of his red eye

and this unrepentant woman
mounts up, clings to wattle
and tendon, leans her ear to his beak

to catch each triangular
syllable tremulous as dawn.
Her doubts burrow

deep into down, she strokes
veins at the base of his throat,
feels the faint tick of faith

just out of reach.
The silty creek of her mind
cannot yet float

that rowboat where some tiny god's
giving one of the chosen
a free ride to the other side.

PHEASANT

This pheasant who roosts
low in the cedars
broke free of the thicket,
strode in full sun
beyond blackberry brambles,
weighted each step,
a dancer pausing
while his costume caught up.

Tense grazer, he pecked quick
beakfuls wild-eyed side to side
every cell alive, too many strides
from cover. His long throat,
deep green of bronze
long left in rain
and sun, his chest
burnished copper.

He walked as if he knew his own worth.
He walked as if he knew
at any moment he could be lifted up
into the gray and fathomless sky
not metaphysically, but by talons
as real as teeth or buckshot.
In spite of that, he walked.

How might it help him
in the wild, his head
the brilliant red of Chinese silk?
It helped us
see him, a flash,
slash across the retina,
gone.

How might this matter
to you, woman on her fourth dose
in the second round of chemo,
woman who no longer counts
on God or statistics,
woman who counts
each hour a winged being,
sharp-clawed, uncaged, poised.

GNAWED BONES

If language is bones, hard parts
of speech, what do skulls of pack rats
crushed into owl pellets
have to tell us?

If this delicate pelvis
once balanced a gravid
javelina, what word passes on
to her shoats?

If cicada shells hang on
like single mothers starved
for touch, what does hot
wind whisper through them?

If every day
re-enacts creation,
if we live
here, now

in the first world
and the last,
let us speak
in our bones

languages of water
from all skies, from
deep underground.
Let our bones quench

the thirst of history,
thirst for all we yearn
to sip, marrow
of each dry tongue.

NESTS, AN ELEGY

In a few seasons,
willows will reinvade

this burn,
slender red shoots

prime browse.
Even scorched

earth provides.
This burn

the size of Phoenix
didn't touch

a single
human house.

But migrants
nest here,

some returning
from Tierra

del Fuego
to this choking

land of fire,
their memories

tribal, alive
in every cell.

They come back,
the goldeneyes

forced to abandon
this year's pale green

clutch in the hollow
just catching.

Buffleheads flare higher,
their nests tinder

twenty feet up.
The marsh hawk's

bowl of dead reeds,
rock ptarmigan's

grass and moss,
the snowy owl's

lichens and feathers
exposed on bare tundra,

the ruffed grouse's
depression lined with leaves,

the great horned owl's
open surface, charred,

the falcon cleared out,
peregrine along

rivers of smoke, blind
but rising, ashes rising.

SMOKE

One hundred thirty moose
in a single pond

suck shallow breaths.
Snarls of black spruce

boom, flash paper, gone.
Two hundred thousand acres,

gray batting.
Air sears.

Wax drips.
Cones that need fire

crack. Seeds
drop while the ash bed's

hot. Shifty wind,
deadly blessing.

WHEN GROUND CANNOT TAKE IN MORE RAIN

Downhill from rare
pines twisted

as sorrow's logic,
the estuary

shines, blocked
but for one bridged river,

turning back on itself
tide by tide.

Those clouds were once
this water on our faces.

Across the moon those clouds
have no doubts. Jostled

by every breeze, every whisper
those clouds have somewhere

to get to, even if
their rain falls

but fails
to reach earth.

Even if
the earth

cannot take in
what they must give.

NIGHT DIVE

Plankton rise toward the full moon
spread thin on Wakaya's surface.
Manta rays' great curls of jaw
scoop backward somersaults of ocean
in through painted caves of their mouths, out
through sliced gills. Red sea fans
pulse. The leopard shark
lounges on a smooth ramp of sand,
skin jeweled with small hangers-on.
Pyramid fish point the way to the surface.

Ninety feet down, blue ribbon eels cough,
their mouths neon cautions.
Ghost pipefish curl in the divemaster's palm.
Soft corals unfurl rainbow polyps, thousands
of mouths held open to night.
Currents' communion—giant clams
slam shut wavy jaws, send
shivers of water. Christmas tree worms
snap back, flat spirals tight,
living petroglyphs against the night.

NIGHT WATCH

Out of sight of land,
our unfinished catamaran climbs
a green swell, six knots uphill
then twenty-six surfing down.

Our postage stamp
upon the ocean, realm with no P.O.
The bilious carpenter's
unglued, heaving at the rail.

Stacking gallon jars
behind sea rails,
the tattooed cook steadies
her globe of merlot

between heads of purple
cabbage, curses
blue flames rollicking,
underworld sneaking up.

Flying fish whipped
out of waves' liquid
moonshadow dry out.
Stars burn through fog

just as the humpback cow
surfaces, her sequined calf
a perfect replica. Twin spires
spume. She gives suck.

We linger in open water,
glad no plot, chart,
or plan built this chance.
Eyes wide,

they watch us
watch them
spiral into our fading
wake. We take

our turns overlooking
the world,
our turns
sounding below.

AS WAR GOES ON

Olive trees do not apologize.
Dusty, their uniforms
drop piece by piece

splattering the sidewalk.
No one can eat such fruit
without curing it in lye.

Brine. Oceans. Eyes.
Overflowing. Paper
beaten from sweat-

stained camouflage
shed by men ready
to be seen,

to speak. From the fountain
fresh waters. Vets beat
to a pulp

loosened fibers,
spread onto screens
the mash of their lives.

Soldiers so young
they've yet to bear
fruit, veterans

so old their roots
tangle, tap
rivers underground.

On the paper
we make of our lives,
what shall we write?

FOR PHIL, HARI, DREW
& ALL MAKERS OF SYMBOLIC PAPER
WWW.IVAW.ORG

BUGLER, FT. WAINWRIGHT, ALASKA

Yellow leaves in July. Damn.
A single osprey banks over birches, cruises
upriver and down. Birch bark splits like the lip
of the bugler hitting a high note
the morning after Tiffany
with a tongue like a mouthful of tadpoles
and a hardhat she neglected
to mention. Gashed knuckles.
He pictures a nicotine chip, his tooth
stuck in an itchy keloid baptized with blood.
No fieldworker with a short-handled hoe
ever had a back that hurt this bad, each vertebra
burnished by fire, each bone a glowing coal, ruby
spine searing inside him. His breath sinks
in and in and in, shriek held back.
Forced through brass his pain
ices over echoed notes of "Taps."

DIVE, THREE DEFINITIONS

dive, n. span of time under water

Seldom more than an hour at a time—the finite number of our breaths—before divers reach 500 psi and have to surface. We know so little of the vast majority of our world, glimpsed through foggy masks and the twin distortions of sloshing water and broken light.

Worldwide, reefs suffer wherever crown-of-thorns starfish take over. The only creature that finds them delicious, the only one that can slip its long foot underneath the crown-of-thorn's formidable armor, flip it, then gorge on the shining delicacies within the star is this: the Trident's Trumpet, prized for the dramatic crenulated whorl of its shell. It's prized almost to extinction, its numbers spiraling down, down. And so the crown-of-thorns star munches in a few weeks corals that take decades to grow, corals that shelter nurseries for damselfish, angels, eels, the small fry the rest of the world depends on. In their wake, hungry stars leave acres of skeletons, bleached.

dive, n. a sleazy bar

e.g., the Boatel, on the south bank of the Chena River, Fairbanks, Alaska, where all summer local drunks minimize their DUIs by firing up their outboards and skimming downriver to the rotting dock. Recently, the Boatel made the paper because it hosted an altercation a little different from the usual bashings and knifings.

In the dank interior, a couple had lost track of how many pitchers they'd downed. They yelled at the TV, "Support our troops, hell yeah. Bring 'em home!"

Two out-of-uniform M.P.s from Fort Wainwright took exception, with fists. The bouncer shoved the M.P.s out back on the deck, the man and woman out front in the parking lot.

The M.P.s saw the couple's boat, knotted to a piling with nylon rope.

The M.P.s got in, untied the leaky inflatable, and headed downriver, toward Pike's, away from the reviewing stand where the ceremony soon would be held. Ceremony for them, ceremony for four thousand Stryker Brigade soldiers about to deploy to Iraq. Half of them leaving for the second time or the third. Their commander's voice—"The enemy wants to hurt our country, hurt our families."

dive, v. 1. to plunge headfirst into water 2. to plummet, to drop sharply

No one paid Harry to take a dive, just one day his leg muscles didn't, when he put weight on them, hold him up. Face-plant on the patio, quick trip to the ER, and Harry started this long descent into the mysteries of the body. Probing with needles, X-rays, magnetic resonance. No dice. Debilitating, the not knowing.

Back home in his recliner, he flicks on the Beijing Olympics. From the 10-meter platform, the best divers in the world flip three times, twist twice, flatten their hands so the surface opens and closes over them with a tiny feather of splash. Harry and I put together a shower chair so he can, without danger, perform his ablutions. Warm water down his back comforts. Especially when he's not clinging to wet tiled walls.

I bring home a sturdy walker that fits him, complete with a seat he can sink into when he tires. We store the rickety frame his wife Suzie pushed for two decades, through not knowing, through lupus, through ovarian cancer, through knowing. Tonight it's synchronized events, athletes perfectly attuned, years of daily practice peaking, if they're lucky, into two forms/one motion. Like the long-married, like Harry and Suzie, their life together never easy. The intense concentration, the consideration of the other, the inevitable plunge.

II. MYSTERY AISLE

Disembodied, the voice from public radio—

Advances in DNA research
require us
to rearrange our collections
to reflect
sharper awareness of
nuance in relationships.

What continues to puzzle us
we place in the mystery aisle.

THE PROVIDER

for my father

Both arms around your waist, I buried
my face in the cracked black
leather of your jacket. The throaty Harley
leaned too far, throttle
cranked, hot pavement chewing up
our foot pegs.
Any stray patch of gravel
suicide. Scabby saguaro
lurched by, lean and wounded,
never young. You loved

pure speed, that bike, and me,
though I had no way
to see it then.
I was fifteen, amazed
at my body and amazed
at you, all six foot six
shutting down with one look
whistles and hot talk
as we eased blinking
out of the desert
into the Beachcomber,
shut down everybody, then turned

for the first time to look at me
not as your elbow or toe
there all the time, easy to bump,
but the woman me, the one so far away
I'd left
before you noticed
I could run.

My showing up
slowed you down, made you trade in
your tunes, your bike, your axe—
your life a down payment on mine.
We both got took.
You soured selling Chevys
and office machines. I took care
of the little kids.

Once, I brought a college friend
to your place. Your fourth wife
sang with you "Bad, Bad Leroy Brown"
and "One Note Samba,"
you clunking along on the clavinet,
those canned drums thumping
like tired pistons.

It was 10:30 in the morning.
A pitcher of salty dogs already
loosened your joints. We sat
on red velvet overstuff
still shrouded in double-duty plastic.
George Wallace, you said.
The only clear choice. I left.

Father, I am ashamed
how ashamed of you
I've always been, when
I know so little
and that little
learned by leaving.

Your absence
has carved in me a place
that healed like a cactus shoe—
hard, fragile, secret—
the deepest gashes
shelter
for some bounding pack rat
or startled cactus wren.

DESERT ODYSSEY

Like us, Telemachus didn't know
where to start
when father didn't come home.

Face down in a field, his mouth
split by stones,
he might need us. We spread out,

hit Tucson Bowl, the Beachcomber,
the Maverick,
listening for his whiskery line

trolling for barflies, pickled
laughter, amber waves—
grain siphoned from bottomless kegs.

TOUCH AND GO

Gone to pick up two dozen
hot from the deep fat
chocolate-frosted,
custard, coconut, cake,

and his favorite, raised and glazed,
he pays cash, swoops up the box
each sweet straight and level
gliding under the lid's window.

Take offs and landings . . .
he makes room on the seat,
moving aside the body
he's built, styrofoam,

engine embedded, taped, wings
detached. At the four-way
stop, his head spirals,
stress cracks, splits.

Nose down breaks the stall
and you'll fly again . . .
He guns it while he
can see, flies low

by trailers, saguaro,
his last turn home,
eases down so smooth
he and the plane are one—

fuel off, flying as long as . . .
he scans for his spot, swallows
two tablets he's heard
can help when blood's

not getting where it needs
to go and blood
rushes free, floods
all emergency

landing strips, old dirt
roads, dry fields,
any flat patch
where he might put down.

ALWAYS THE ENTERTAINER

Flat on his back in emergency, he
tries to get me
to laugh. He's breathing
sporadically, he's clammy.

"He's very sick," the ER doc
tells me. As if I couldn't
see that for myself.
I stroke Dad's arm, cold

to the touch. He says,
"Have you heard the one . . ."
and here it comes
racist, crass, unfunny

again this joke sick with toe-maine
he's told in some version, knee-monia
all my life dick-theria
I've cringed.

The most I can muster
is a grimace, steady look
right in his eyes
where I see

he knows how close
this call really is.
He's tap dancing
for all he's worth

not sure
at all
what it is
he's worth.

To the overworked attending
he brags on me,
grabs onto that swinging vine,
aaaah-UH-ah-UH-aaah—our tangled jungle.

RINSING THAT TOMATO

Sunwarm in my palm, the heft—
summer's first juice-heavy

ripeness snapped
from its hairy vine.

On his deathbed
my father

needed to hear
how proud

I was of him
and I couldn't

wouldn't shouldn't didn't
lie. My touch,

gentle, the kind
that wouldn't bruise.

Two hands,
open-palmed, cool

water rinsing away
flecks of our ancestors, us,

and soon enough
our proud children.

YOU'RE HERE

He closes
his huge hand over hers,
drawing her close.

"I've been alone four days."
He's confined
behind rails,

in a bed that lifts
feet or head but not
his heart, sure now

that if he knew then
what he knows now
he'd never have come

never have let her call
never have left
his chair where

he realized how completely
something'd gone
wrong, chair where

he was last himself, chair
where he'll never
settle again. "Four days,"

he says. "By myself."
"I know," she says, "But
I'm here now." Tired

woman who has not left
his side, woman
unshowered, stiff

from dropping off
in the bedside chair,
woman who knows

he's right, her man
who mistook her
for his mother

late in the night,
child again in the dark
alone her husband

who's been somewhere
she can't go
with him,

husband headed somewhere
she can't go
with him, husband.

CHICKENS

All blasted night you fretted, knew
they were outside the wire, your mother's
whole flock, the reds and the plumper
whites, scratching for pillbugs curled up
tight, your body lithe as you ran
through the garden, careful of strawberries
ripe on pallets of mulch,
careful of staked tomatoes
and teepees of sweet peas,
of butterbeans waxing full as moons.

Then the sun came up. The moon faded
down to its daytime self. You were returned
though you never quite believed it
and how could you to this half life
in your half shell, left side limp,
unsure which side of the story
was yours, what you had left
hard to tell, the loneliness of seeing
what everyone else couldn't yet
see. Candling those eggs.

SWALLOWS

That moment not dusk but just before—

The earth turned away a bit more
from the sun, last shadows not long
for this land. Our steps disturbed
tiny winged creatures who risked
their lives to fly ankle high
late glimmers rising so
sleek fork-tailed
swoop-winged swallows
whipped through, snicked up
beak after beak full of ticking.

Those moments inside us we don't for years
comprehend, until the morning
miles away when we pretend
it's important to spoon into a helpless elder
a little peach yogurt and he pretends
clean now after a kind Ukrainian
stranger has bathed him in bed
that swallowing whatever's on the held spoon
might be how he'd choose to spend
the last moments left him.

He swallows twice the strained
yogurt, twice sips of honey-thick
nectar, then spits the straw,
bright-eyed. *I'll swallow*
three times if I want to. Grins.
Swallows for good
every last word.

Those moments hand in hand,
his eyes on mine, when what he utters
I can't understand.

Swallow. Twice. Again.

HA HA HA

More than once before you had fooled us, taken time off
from breathing, a showman's pause drawn out
longer than was wise, longer than the crowd could bear

then taken us all in with that ragged
rasp, what the lung man called Cheyne-Stokes,
a pattern of leaving and returning

then huffing hard to make up
for whatever you left behind
all those years. Your chest stayed still.

Your hand in my hand, warm
still. Your eyes a color I'd not seen
closed as if finally

you had escaped and no one ever
again could hold you
responsible, your last joke.

NO SIGN

One generation passeth away, and another generation cometh.
~Ecclesiastes 1:4

Just moments after your death,
a young woman, very young, knocks
then peeks

around the hospital door
I'd closed.
"I clean now?" She smiles,

ready to make our world
better. I blurt
"My father has died."

Deep wells, her eyes,
water she doesn't hide.
"Mi padre también."

And we're in each other's
worlds right then, in each other's
arms, found in this translation.

* * *

Perky, used to coaxing
half-conscious or deeply ill
folks without appetites,

the dietician
breezes in.
"Ready to choose

your dinner,
Mister . . .

... And then she sees.

* * *

His wife's daughters arrive,
take their turns
kissing his forehead,

the only father
they've known
lo these many years.

Then two strapping
young men swagger in,
snapping on latex gloves

and start to touch him.
"Why are you here?" I whisper.
"To turn him,"

they declare, confident,
reaching. "You're aware
my father has died?"

Both recoil
as if they hadn't suspected
such a thing existed

within their realm,
back out
filling the still air

with their young
men's stuttered
apologies

MY FATHER NEVER

My father never
hit us, never
noticed
if we'd been bad
or good, never
knew our favorite
foods or what we hated.

He complained
Those divorces wiped me out,
hangdog, ashamed,
as if all the bad stuff
dropped on him,
he never
had a thing
to do with it.

My father never
lost his wanderlust
his need
to break free, never
spent money
on a decent pair
of shoes.

My father never
walked comfortably
on this earth.

Always the tallest,
my father never chose
to bounce drunks
out of dingy bars,
never rose to the bait
of short-guy taunts.

My father never
broke through
my sister's Great Wall—
violent ice
need stacked on need,
unmet. She shoved him
away, while she wanted him
closer, wanted
him to know
how to be
family.

My father never
had a feeding tube
stuck in his belly.
His wish, respected,
though my sister fought
for it, wanting
what?
after his stroke
so massive
even things the body does
without thinking
stuttered, faltered,
couldn't carry on.

BEYOND WORDS, THIS LANGUAGE

The morning I was born
         you held my hand.

The morning you died
         I held your hand.

What's left
         to forgive?

RADIO CONTROL

After your friends testified
how when they stroked on the pinstripes,
chose the call numbers, balanced
engine, body, and landing gear

when all that work was ready
for the virgin flight, they
brought it to you, the new craft,
to see what it could do.

They knew you'd ease it up
into the air, anticipating
rough ground, rough
air, compensating

for whatever they hadn't
thought of, whatever
wouldn't show up
until wind rushed over the wings

and the perfect angle of attack
lifted it off into the blue
for a turn or two over the trailer park
above cacti and creosote

slipping on the crosswind
easing back to hard-baked
earth, and the huge sigh
when it touched down, safe

on earth. After that
while your daughter choked
on words she'd scrawled
to honor you, above us all

came the whining hum
your craft out of sight
wing and roar
sailing over.

NO ONE KNOWS HOW TO SPEAK

Quiet scours the sky.
Unspoken for some time,
words of the disappeared

return to us, songs
jokes wisdom warnings
return to us, whole

languages blurry, laughter
twisted, obliterated. Tears
so constant our generation

assumes they're language,
drunks postholing through snow
along Two Street, tracking

fur-bearing quarry that fed
elders long ago, fed
old ones remembered still

by name, fed us with
dreams of a future
we could not imagine

and here it is, we're living it
now stripped bare,
not much to say.

ALBÓNDIGAS

In clear broth
among bits of rice
float little worlds

rolled between
her palms,
globes spiced

with cominos, ajo,
cilantro, cebolla,
simmered

in fresh caldo
for us this time
albóndigas

just the way
he liked it,
my father

who just months
before his death
hit us up for a loan

we could have his pension
all he wanted was
a motorhome

he figured out
they just didn't fit—
Incompatible!

so could we work something out
he had to get out
he'd like to get

out on the road
just find a spot
where he could play

a few tunes, tell a few jokes,
have a drink
when he felt like it . . .

We didn't float him
the loan. We offered a place
he could take some time.

Two weeks later
he gassed up his car, drove home,
gassed up hers like always.

She can't stand to pull up
to the pump, she tells us,
can't stand that smell.

He always did that
my sweet baby
that was his job

she says, glancing
up at the glass
top of the curio

cabinet, her eyes
lingering, the dark
blue velvet bag

shrouding the box
holding the few
heavy bits she has left.

PORTAL

My father's fifth wife was the only one he really married. The others were legal, sure. But they weren't binding. Maybe his fifth wife was so thoroughly married he had to be, too. Concepción Álvarez Sotelo Howe. His true mate, Connie. For the last quarter century of his life, she taught my father to be part of a family. Hers. Everybody on her side casually called my father Grandpa. His own grandkids rarely saw him, and referred to him, in his absence, as "Your Dad." Connie tried hard to include us, four grown kids he'd failed to raise, but we'd already scattered, dust kicked up by Dad's tires, leaving leaving leaving leaving.

After mourning him for one year, Connie punched a door through the dining room wall of their trailer, scraped gravel back to bare dirt. She cooked up a huge pot of albóndigas, his favorite, galaxies of tiny planets floating among yerba buena and arróz. 'Tis the season—she decorated eleven trees. One with thimble-sized teacups, eye-sized saucers. One with miniature ballet slippers, lace-up boots, sequined spike heels. Red hats and purple boas festooned one little pine. The space between cupboards and ceiling she crammed with plastic poinsettias, fake holly. We sipped broth from gold-toned spoons, down to the Santa faces grinning in our bowls. We sipped lemonade from snowflake glasses. Where did she stash this stuff the rest of the year?

Three hefty grandsons shoveled and shoveled. Out the back of Elvia's red pickup a lush Carolina cherry reclined, out of place in this climate. The grandsons borrowed a pick, hacked through hard pack. They walked the tree, roots bound in wood, to the edge of the pit, snapped metal straps, peeled back punky planks. The squared roots backslid to dirt.

If those branches grow wider, even a foot, she won't be able to walk outside. Maybe that's the point. Maybe when it's cool enough, she'll leave the door open and breathe him in, breeze through the leaves.

Connie's great-grandkids swiped licorice, chased whoever ran. Zoe pointed—What's that on your chin? A mole, my husband Joe told her. Want to see a really big one? He pulled aside his collar, let her touch the eerie darkness. Adults agile enough perched on the curb. Murmuring elders unfolded webbed chairs, settled into shadows under awnings.

Without ceremony, without comment, Connie drew down the blue velvet bag, slit open the box, snipped the cord. Without a word she poured through earth's portal silky streams. His silver coated her fingers. Half she held back to mix into mountains he loved.

Flecks of bone dappled wet dirt. Ragged molecules of our dead, dispersed.

Silent, we tossed in words folded over, notes unsung. Sealed now, they hum at the root of what may or may not thrive in the desert.

III. *OUR MOTHER OF SORROWS*

LAND FRAUD NOSEBLEED

We'd be out in the desert
fifteen miles from Fort Huachuca
checking out the latest

bogus development—street
signs tilting in caliche,
no water, no electricity,

just salesmen yapping
like freshly groomed poodles
and my strapped parents nodding

nodding but never talking,
never signing, just polite
till the Mexican cooks

opened the pit
and FREE BBQ smoke
watered our eyes and mouths.

Right then, on cue,
my mother would glance over
just as my nose flooded,

blots big as summer raindrops
staining my crop top and shorts,
and the salesmen running up

with Dixie cups of crushed
ice, almost heaven
if I didn't hold it

too long
to the bridge
of my nose . . .

Then plates of shredded
beef and pinto beans, green
chilies and white bread

appeared like mirages—
plenty, enough, too much
so we ate

what we could,
said thanks, really,
foiled the rest

and balanced
paper plates on
bare knees

all the way, tissues
mashed to my tilted-back
face, getting away

with it,
all the way
home.

Saguaros tied up
in surveyor's tape,
cacti packing heat,

held their own seeds
hostage on high,
Apache tears packed buckshot tight.

The cracker box trailer-office got
hauled off to the next patch
of creosote and jumping cactus.

The dirt stayed. Trash
hung around, blew off
with dust devils, snagged

on barb wire. Before the heat
of the day, uprooted Yaqui
women whose third language

tasted metallic,
sharp blades of English
on the tongue, rose,

lifted saguaro ribs
and ocotillo spikes
to whap down

fruit out of reach.
They picked up those strong enough
not to split,

left behind those broken,
bleeding
into a new generation.

DESERT CLIMBING

Knee-scraping up the big mesquite
bark cracks oozing amber
sap so sticky our palms, our arms
wore for days dirt-dusted tracks,
we knew we'd pay.

Picking between wicked stickers,
rattling bean pods shrunken dry,
we'd settle on branches
a little too fragile
to bear our weight. Sky high,

invisible among feathery green,
we'd whisper our secrets,
knots we had to grow around.
Under bark flakes, red ants
conducted their lives,

stung constellations
onto our thighs,
retreated into small cities
underground, their powdery
anthills perfect, dry.

BETTER HOMES

Under the scarred palo verde
on the playground at Mother of Sorrows
in bare dirt between goatheads

we dragged scuffed heels,
scraping up houses,
places we'd rather live.

Bean pods rattled among white spikes,
green lizard bark.
Patio, carport, bedroom, kitchen,

driveway, hallway,
private bath.
All the rooms of our living

we dug in.
Damn! Don't walk through my walls!
You cussed. I'm telling.

Go ahead.
Just proves
you're too little.

We built our houses on powder,
on dirt uncommitted
to any one place,

dream homes that lasted
days, moments, hours.
We heard

before we saw
dust devils whooshing,
ducked into postures

every desert kid knows—
squat on heels,
face buried

in elbow, eyes
squinched tight
against the grit,

sharp dirt
stinging
bare skin—

dust devils ripped
over under
around and through,

erasing every door,
every window,
howling like divorce.

GO TO THE BROOM CLOSET AND PICK OUT A STICK

Fish sticks and french fries.
Beans and wieners and instant
potatoes. Red goop. Gray goop.
Don't tell me Mom couldn't cook.
Allemande left with your left hand.
With her glasses off, Mom never heard
a word we said. She had us
convinced. She could see
through walls, around
corners. She could hear
what we were thinking.
We were afraid
she could see our secrets
even from her grave.
Make the world
go away,
get it ah-off
my sho-ol-der.
Mirror lost, she couldn't signal.
Ladies Center Back to the Bar.
Hinge and Flutter. Flare the Star.
Off-key, she rasped
from the depths of her sinuses
songs, spelunkers.
Swing your partner,
right and left grand.
Raw gash, Grand Canyon the same age
as geological loneliness, her
bones. Ancient oceans.
Slot canyons twisted
inside her,
worn down
by what ran through.
What do I know of her loneliness?

HORNY TOADS

Vodka bottles
stashed in the ragbag

torn-out knees
in pajamas with feet

her daughter
never took off,

too small
in winter, cut off

in summer,
four grubby seasons.

Palo verde bent back
white spines scraping green skin,

writing in languages
no one alive

could speak, palo verde
bent back, pliable

feathers velvety
as the drunken tongue

we waited for her
to outgrow, silent

as horny toads
leathery bellows

burrowed into
brick-hard earth.

ASTHMA

The reason she couldn't swim, couldn't
push us on swings.
The reason we moved away
from the sea into the desert.
The reason one whole cupboard rattled with her pills.
The reason palo verde in bloom
sent her careening to St. Joe's. The reason I sat close,
grabbed the wheel when her lips turned blue.
The reason she hugged so hard.
The reason no animal found refuge in her lap.
The reason she stashed
vodka bottles in the ragbag.
The reason she yelled,
"Go to the broom closet and pick out
a stick." The reason smoke
filled her eyes. The reason
mournful cowboy songs riddled her.
The reason her first breaths
in the morning scraped and clattered like rusty
hay balers.

The reason she couldn't carry a tune
in a bushel basket with a lid.
The reason she sang anyway.
The reason at sunset in her throat her husband
kick-started his Harley, spit gravel behind him
as he peeled out. The reason her laugh—sheet lightning—
cracked the sky. The reason she picked through
spaghetti she didn't make herself.
The reason she quit eating.
The reason she loved quiet
more than her own kids. The reason quiet never entered her
body, never entered her mind. The reason she didn't want to
be here. The reason she left. The reason we buried her
under a stone with no last name.

Her wings weren't always orange. Nor her face aqua. The pressure in her skull arced left to right from the arch of one ear to the other. Her right ear went deaf, her left eye dark. But by the time the contestant spun the wheel for the bonus round, the clacking brought her back to where she could see Pat Sajak guiding a third grade teacher to her sweet spot, outlined on the studio floor. Masking tape. She couldn't be sure what was going on inside her own head. Scans pretended to slice her brain so thin any fool could see right through her. The blank spots, whitened by mystery, mattered to her. The rubber band used to wrap twice around her waist-length hair. Four times now. Coiled mat every morning over the drain. At night she counted scorpions clawing inside her walls. Her wings kept her awake all summer, wouldn't fold right. Bare ground too hot to walk on.

SKY OF SOULS

Trembling at the edges, the night sky's
not wide enough—northern lights
breeze beyond rolling horizons,

scalloped hills, the simple
curve of our earth.
A soul learns nothing

while a soul. The deepest spirals
baptize our eyes in lights,
dip into the beautiful black

mouth of mystery. And the souls
feel it, the not-knowing
they cannot bear, they love

questions so much.
A holy man
once told me

a child can atone
for her mother's death
wish. Beneath these soul-spiked

lights I believe
he might be right.
I shall atone

each time I breathe
these lights,
each time I listen

to beings I cannot see,
each time I open myself
trembling

at the edges,
lighting the whole wide
whirling sky.

UPSET WOMAN

—after a drawing by Florence Napaaq Malewotkuk

Napaaq drew in ink
the sure lines of anguish,
a young woman nearly naked
weeping so hard her hands
could not hide her, her hands
could not hold this grief
passed down by the mothers,
the grandmothers, the ones so old
only stories could hold them.

This woman is young, young enough
to swallow all the sadness
passed down to her, to make it
her own. Her lover, a white man
with a thousand promises
in his misunderstanding advises her
and so she letters with great care
a caption in his language:

*Some men hate his wife 'cause she love other men. That why he hate her
she crying now. She naked body. Pretty-soon love together again.*

As if each tear has nothing
to do with the ocean,
with the drowned, nothing
to do with passing on
to a newborn
the names of the most recent
dead, who still walk around
to see how we think,
what we say, how we feel.

YOU SHOULD KNOW BETTER

Nobody, no matter how starved
for touch, looks forward
to a pelvic
exam. Nobody sings
zippedy-do-dah
with her feet in stirrups,
even stirrups
cozied up in oven mitts.

She warms the speculum,
my good doctor, warns me
before each touch.
And still I jump
a little, push back
from the edge
a little, close my eyes
to interrogation,
no parts private
under probing lights.

I try to see this
as routine. Spritz
fixes cells
swabbed from my cervix
onto glass slides,
their testimonies invisible
to the naked eye.

One gloved hand inside
she slides the warm other
skin to skin over my abdomen.
This year she stops. Checks again.

Waits till I dress
to say to my face

Tumor.
I stutter,
What b-brings them on?
and she says, professional
as ever, *Dirty thoughts,*
usually.
Well, no wonder.

This weird cellular stuff's
passed down and down,
generations.
Nobody in my family
ever breathed a word.
I call my grandmother,
blurt, What do you know
about hysterectomies?
and she says, I only had
one. One's all you get,
you know.

What's the etiquette?
I ask to see it,
whatever they take out,
curious about
what has come to live in me,
curious too to see in person
what I've known
mostly from sketches—
instructions tucked inside
the Tampax box,
The Visible Woman, her layers
peeled back, Our Bodies,
Ourselves, and once
in the '70s a practitioner's
purple hand mirror
held so I could see.

Groggy after surgery
thumbing the pain button
like a contestant on Jeopardy
What is morphine?
I imagine never moving again.
Each swell of pain
crests, rolls on.
The thread
stitching me together
dissolves.

Of course they found things
they hadn't counted on.
Of course my beloved
kissed the scar.

And because I asked,
they showed me
my Fallopian tubes
sturdy as heater hoses.
My cervix knobby as a punched
nose. Slashed tire
womb. The tumor
that grew inside
heavy, a shot put,
but marbled, muscular,
my secret unscathed heart.
And the bonus tumor
growing on a stalk,

odd yellow,
yolk of all my eggs
never ripened into children,
renegade ovary,
releasing all through me
fugitive colors.

GLYPHS ON A LIMESTONE STELA

Jumping was forbidden, so I dove.
Fell, fell, half a lifetime.

Cliffside to cenote, full twist
showing off my best sides.

Evelia's eyes cenote verde
her laugh a cascade clean and cool.

Third time for sure she was watching,
third time oiled and glinting,

steel drum lucky, I lifted—
feet slipped earth and I flew

over papaya, mango, fruta de sueños.
My tongue yerba buena, buena suerte

a new reed, moistened.
Canción.

     Detour
mid-air.

     Gravity side

swiped me.

Her tongue traced the crease
of my eyelid, dreamy.

Small bones in a back.
Water I never broke.

ALL THE MUSTACHES ON ALL THE JUDASES

Hairs from the base of the tail
of a striped cat fed on lard

touch up both flourishes
(the liberal / the old guard)

of Judas's mustache.
All the mustaches on all the Judases

lashed to firecrackers
the night before Easter

blast into Kingdom Come
or the next day at least

when we see what one kiss
ordains—that betrayal

reveals the soul,
stands us naked

in the spotlight.
One kiss—lit fuse!

Then the brain-blasting
strobe of owning up.

***Though outlawed in 1957, the practice during
Holy Week of each family destroying an effigy of
Judas continues in Mexico and Central America.
Many of the artists who create Judas figures also
make skeletons in action for Day of the Dead.*

THE AROMA OF RAIN IN THE DESERT

Rain so brief
dust puffs up,
each drop
a small hollow
moist as a secret
held under the tongue.

Black and yellow
buzzing sexual,
wide open
false eyes,
mariposa wings
not quite dry.

Each drop bursts—bright orange
poppies erupt, flow
molten down the flanks
of Picacho, hot
ocean of small hands
waving from under earth.

MANGO

Handful of ripe mango
heavy with juice
I balance, guessing
where to slice
so the knife might
just scrape by
the flat face of the pip.

If I guess wrong
forgive me anyway,
grandmother offering
stories for breakfast.

OCOTILLO

Candlewood
spread with palm fronds—

strong ramadas.
Mean fences, sprouting

new spines
overnight.

Slimwood. Bare
most every month

except after rain
when each pore

spurts green gloss
and the tip

of every arm
in the desert

explodes into salsa.
Firecrackers.

Jacob's staff.
Flaming sword.

Many-armed
hope. Ocotillo.

NORWEGIAN WOOD

By the time I scored an almost-mint *Hard Day's Night* poster for fifteen cents at the swap meet, nobody plastered her walls anymore with John, Paul, George, Ringo. Survival cliques weren't formed anymore by girls who thought Ringo was cutest. He wasn't. But those girls would never fit in with Paul's group or John's and they knew it. Nobody wore Beatles tennis shoes—our toes had long since poked through.

Under my madras shift, I hid my necklace—inch-high leather binder that unsnapped to reveal accordion-pleated Fab Four portraits, zigzag snapshots. We didn't suffer anymore the unbearable wonder about how a boy's hand might feel on our skin, slipping under shirttails deliberately not tucked in, then traveling the vast unmapped wilderness of our bodies. Seismic upthrusts. Protruded nipples shiny as Paul's front teeth. Womb ache thick as Liverpool accents. Eight days a week the boys we knew counted on us to keep their balls blue no matter how hard they sang love, love me do.

MOTHER TONGUE

In a language recently
disappeared, god
is talking.

No one knows anymore
how long the leaves
keep silent

how deep
the stones' truth
lies buried

what silent kinship
glints off blond fur
where grizzly cubs graze.

In the far time, nearly
everyone could speak
with salmon,

water,
clouds, stars.
Every body.

Now no one sees the ocean
though it lives in every tear.

In a language lost to us
god is singing.

THAT PAINTING I DIDN'T BUY

Late afternoon in Jerome,
ghost town turned
artsy, I saw this painting.

A purple horse bent
his head low to catch wisps
of a woman's voice, she

bent her face
away, I couldn't
see her eyes, turned

her mouth
toward the open ear
velvety to her touch.

I stepped closer as if
to overhear
what she might choose

to say, secrets
shared but
not revealed

the horse having no one
to talk to
no one

to betray. My friends
ready to move on
shuffled out

only slightly
skittish, their shoes
echoing on the board

sidewalk. Had the purple
horse been mine,
I might over the years

have forgotten to look
into her eyes, neglected
to listen

for secrets
never meant
for me.

Whispered
brushstrokes—
had they

been free, I
would have had
to make payments.

So instead, I took them
in, breathed
with them woman

and horse,
background, landscape—
inside me still, this life.

IV. NAMING WHAT WE HOLD
IN OUR HAND

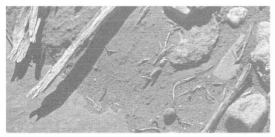

WILDERNESS

The voice yelling in the wilderness
doesn't know what year it is
doesn't know how old it is
doesn't know its own name

The voice pleading in the wilderness
can't recall how it got here
doesn't know where this is
can't locate its hands

The voice echoing in the wilderness
can't guess how many fingers or why
no matter how intensive the care
doesn't know it's married to silence

PALE WOMAN ON STRETCHER

Before the tube choked off words, I spoke.

To my husband I said what might be the last.

I barely understood what they intended, only that they wanted

desperately to help. After the first numbing, I fought.

After the second, my resisting, instinctive, was no match

for their gentleness. For forty-five minutes an aide squeezed

plastic bulb-fuls of air into my lungs.

Weeks later, reading dictated notes, I find out

a machine breathed for me for two days.

Where are they, those days?

Where are those days that slip away surely as breath?

WHAT NEXT

Lungs saddled up
for the embolus express

I am the nightmare.
Who is my rider?

Of all those who've gone before
could it be

the one I most
long to see?

Or, packhorse
overloaded,

am I lugging
heavy as slump blocks

strapped to my chest
all the children

I never nursed?
Spurring me

down the stretch,
let it be you

you, my love,
and gravid curiosity.

A BRIEF ASIDE

Later you tell me
how they cut off my clothes,
snipped right through the front
of my bra, stuffed the scraps
into a plastic bag with a handle,
and absurdly presented it to you.

Things were moving fast.
Flat on the gurney on the way to surgery
I opened one eye.
You remembered what it takes
for me to see.
Nobody there knew how to help this time,
so you whispered in my ear.

I don't recall
reaching up
and deftly, with my left hand,
plucking out
what brought the blurry
world into focus.

NARROW ROADS TO/FROM THE INTERIOR

Tubes get the scut work:

The Foley hoards a pot of gold
at the end of the rein.

Twin bulbs, like garlic,
swell with blood
no vampire gets near.

A hidden pump
wet/dry shop vac
mucks out the lungs.

That odd tongue
licks up over the patella,
kisses the bent spot
to make it better.

Above, patient
as erosion, as torture,
the IV drop by drop
reveals what we're really made of.

MISSING

Coming around,
one eye circling,
I can't tell whether death
hurts this much, or
whether breath
this measured
is a bad joke,
taken in by machines.

Blank spots dot
my brain. Beneath staples,
no spleen. What else
is missing?
The impact,
done & gone, nowhere
to be seen.

My own edges, sharpened
by pain dulled by morphine,
morphing. Long days
my loved ones
treaded rough water
while I floated,
face down.

Ice cold lemonade
I scrawl, and Joe
dips the swab in ice chips.
I need to wash these smells
off my body. I need to cut away
the snarled mess
so my head can rest, level.

STROKES

Whether painter's sable or flogger's lash
each slash is meant
to stay, to mark the moment
and to live on, bearing witness
to all who see the scar
whether or not they understand
where it came from,
brush or bullwhip.

Bubble or clot, hard block
stopping blood to the brain,
blanks out territories
that won't be heard from
again, blanks out
the middle of a sentence,
the whole family
of words, paints over
whole passages
of a marked life,
memorable to those
marked out, remarkable.

LAPSE

What happened to us?

I watch him draw in
a deep breath.

I know then I've asked and asked
many times. And he has answered.
He gathers himself, trying hard.
What could he say that would stay heard?

HARD STICK

Every sharp inquiry
comes up dry.

Blood turns shy.
Veins shut

so far down
doctors can't touch

a pulse.
They hold

their breath,
listen. Again.

As if it suspects
it doesn't contain

infinite secrets
or any, lately,

the body holds on
to what it can.

SPLEEN

Who needs angels?
I have avenging nieces,
who have taken biology

and believe true justice
compels them
to track down

the kid screaming illegally
down the bike path,
four-wheel ATV blind

behind brush,
split seconds before
he tossed our lives like dice.

The avenging nieces reason
it's only fair—
a spleen for a spleen—

They're pretty sure
once they've got him
open, they can pick his out

and once removed
seal it in a Mason jar,
unvented for posterity.

SHOWER

When you have traveled to the edge,
looked over, pulled back,
when a machine has drawn breath
for you for a day, for two,
when your bruises, travel stickers
for trips you don't remember,
haven't faded, but you've come back,
back to some sense of self,
what do you want?

First, a shower. You cannot
believe the stench near death,
how it clings. But you have to get
a special dispensation,
and help. The doc says all right,
just not too hot. It's slow,
leaning down the hallway on Joe,
the IV stand tangling. The shower
has thank god a chair, but no
handheld head. Inhuman
strength this will take.
No. Just more than you've got.

Aiming the body
toward water,
you take no breath
for granted.
Aiming
toward water
the body. Aiming
toward cleansing
toward breath.

GOOD SIGN

I hobble to the window
glad to see, though it's blurry,
the river.

Dark slash tipped with white
swoops through the blue.
An eagle, look! I cry.

I'm leaning on Hanna.
She sees it, too. *Get real.*
That's a raven with a biscuit.

NAMING WHAT WE HOLD IN OUR HAND

Penny.
Paperclip.

Key.
Rubber band.

So far
the signals

from fingertips
to brain

to lips,
wild leaps

electrical
chemical.

What could be
more simple?

Until the day
we cannot

do it.
What then

do we hold
in our hand?

Secret lives
unspoken

names
of everyday

things. The doctor
of missed connections

waits.
The least injured

part of me
wants to look him

straight in the soul
and identify

by touch alone
what our hands hold

shooting star
red aurora

mist forest
life after this

life.

KUS-SUN-AR

For an injured friend,
he brings salmon fillets, fish
he caught dipnetting all night at Chitina.
Needle-nose pliers nipped out
all the invisible bones.

Growing up at fish camp, he'd sneeze.
Elders said, "Kus-sun-ar."
Otter. They invoked otter's name
to wish him close
to one who lives in more than one world.
Shaman helper, on land, in water.

He tells me otters live inside women, curled up
just above the stomach,
and this feels true. I feel my otters,
restless, disturbed.

My hurt body can't rest yet,
it was so close to the other world.

I'm an otter, skinned in the round,
my pelt pulled off in one piece.
Stitched into a kit bag,
I feel the shaman
feeding me salmon,
placing his healing
into my emptiness.

OATMEAL

Dry slide of Bob's Red Mill
Extra Thick Rolled Oats
off the scoop—

tiny dustcloud
settling like ash
from stirred coals.

Waking together,
happy, not
our first try.

IN PRAISE, EPHEMERA

At dawn feeding swans, upended
by the ice shelf, black beaks
champing half-thawed weeds,

draw us to the riverbank. Grizzled feathers,
echo of boots over rotting snow. Far between,
few, tundra swans step out on late ice.

Glacial melt, snow melt
hustle downstream—
ice dams hold tight

jostled swathes of half-lace ice.
Knife-edged narrow
leads open, sliced river swollen.

Muskrat and beaver gnaw
new shoots of red willow,
open winter lodges. Fresh water, air.

Pollen, lavish, carpets the
quick and the dead, blessing the
revived, blessing the remade.

Season of cold broken. Season of ice broken. Season of
tattered shirtsleeves. Bare hands
useful again after burrowing all winter.

Voles gather first shoots of new grasses,
weave fresh sheaves to put by, chew new roots, shoots, and
xylem, drunk on the season's sugars risen

yesterday and today, this hour
zipping by, lifting off, wild swan in clear sky.

CHATANIKA

High, the Chatanika,
high this year, surges
the flats, soaks
the valley. Chatanika

spreads wide
where gravel braids.
Where banks
snug close,

where rock,
earth, and root
gang up, high water
scours, carves,

its own image
changeable.
Chatanika, in pools
deep green, in eddies

steeped tea, freezes
and thaws, makes its way on,
full of grayling
flashing like thoughts

among the millions
of mirrors at Minto.
*What brought me
exactly here?*

*Is my flowing
through the world
a fit gift? Have I nourished
more roots than I undercut?*

LONG BEFORE WE GOT HERE,
LONG AFTER WE'RE GONE

In the season blue-white sun
barely lifts above the ridge,
limps along the horizon
then dives out of sight,
we're changed each day by light.

Someone who's gone before
broke trail, set tracks.
With the right kick wax,
we make our way among birch
breathing hard rare frosted light.

We make of light arpeggio crystals,
caribou dance fans, shush
of bristles. One moment made
alive, human, unafraid.
All that's lost not gone.

ACKNOWLEDGMENTS

Many thanks to the editors and publishers who first welcomed this work, sometimes in different versions.

Alaska Quarterly Review: "Bugler, Ft. Wainwright, Alaska," "What Next"

The American Poetry Review: "Chatanika," "Wilderness"

Arizona Highways: "Ocotillo"

Ascent: "Pale Woman on Stretcher," "A Brief Aside," "Narrow Roads to/from the Interior," "Missing," "Lapse," "Hard Stick," "Shower," "Good Sign," "That Painting I Didn't Buy"

Blackbird: "Deliverance," "Kus-sun-ar"

The Book of Words, Sarabande. "Dive, Three Definitions"

canwehaveourballback?: "Pheasant"

Copper Nickel: "Long Before We Got Here, Long After We're Gone," "Our Mother of Sorrows"

Crab Creek Review: "What We Get Used To"

Crab Orchard Review: "Smoke," "Nests, An Elegy"

Crazyhorse: "Land Fraud Nosebleed"

Flyway: "Polished Table"

The Gettysburg Review: "Chickens," "Ha Ha Ha," "No Sign"

International Journal of Healthcare and Humanities: "Gnawed Bones," "No Sign"

The Iowa Review: "Oatmeal," "Strokes"

Junctures (New Zealand): "Polished Table"

Manoa: "The Provider"

Poetry Kantu (Japan): "When Ground Cannot Take in More Rain"

Prairie Schooner: "Desert Odyssey," "Touch and Go," "Always the Entertainer," "Rinsing that Tomato," "Radio Control," "Upset Woman," "In Praise, Ephemera," "Glyphs on a Limestone Stela," "You Should Know Better"

Salt River Review: "All the Mustaches on All the Judases," "Horny Toads"

Seattle Review: "Naming What We Hold In Our Hands"

Spirituality and Health: "July Twilight on the Chena"

Thanalonline: "Beyond Words, This Language"

Water~Stone: "Portal"

Weber Studies: "Mother Tongue"

"Oatmeal" was included in *Poetry Daily Essentials* 2007, Diane Boller and Don Selby, editors, and also in the *Seren* anthology *Women's Work*, featuring writers from the UK, US, NZ and Australia, Amy Wack and Eva Salzman, editors.

Verse Daily Monthly Feature, "Deliverance"

A letterpress broadside printed by Heather Neal Kasvinsky, with painting "Bright Tracks" by Kesler Woodward, features "Long Before We Got Here, Long After We're Gone." Broadside was part of the Alaska State Council on the Arts 2009 Alaska Arts and Culture Conference.

"In Praise, Ephemera" was exhibited at the Chicago Cultural Center as part of Collaborative Visions: the Poetic Dialogues Project. I collaborated with visual artist Laura Ann Cloud.

Prose versions of some of this material appeared in *Just Breathe Normally*, University of Nebraska Press, 2007.

Thank you to the many friends who offered help, sustenance, laughter.

BOOKS BY PEGGY SHUMAKER

Poetry

Esperanza's Hair

The Circle of Totems

Wings Moist from the Other World

Braided River (chapbook)

Underground Rivers

Blaze (with paintings by Kesler E. Woodward)

Greatest Hits (chapbook)

Gnawed Bones

Memoir

Just Breathe Normally